Wellbeing:
It's Up to Us!

Sally Cowan

Wellbeing: It's Up to Us!

Text: Sally Cowan
Publishers: Tania Mazzeo and Eliza Webb
Series consultant: Amanda Sutera
 Hands on Heads Consulting
Editor: Holly Proctor
Project editors: Annabel Smith and
 Jarrah Moore
Designer: Leigh Ashforth
Project designer: Danielle Maccarone
Permissions researcher: Helen Mammides
Production controller: Renee Tome

Acknowledgements
We would like to thank the following for permission to reproduce
copyright material:

Front cover, p. 25: iStock.com/max-kegfire; pp. 1, 15: iStock.com/Morsa
Images; pp. 3, 5 (bottom): iStock.com/real444; p. 4: iStock.com/
DGLimages; p. 5 (top): Shutterstock.com/NDAB Creativity; p. 6: Getty
Images/Imgorthand; p. 7: Shutterstock.com/beats1; p. 8: Shutterstock.
com/Lopolo; p. 9 (top): iStock.com/monkeybusinessimages, (bottom):
Shutterstock.com/BearFotos; p. 10: iStock.com/vorDa; p. 11: iStock.
com/ATHVisions; p. 12: iStock.com/FatCamera; p. 13: iStock.com/
Imgorthand; p. 14: iStock.com/AzmanL; p. 16 (top): Shutterstock.
com/ADDICTIVE STOCK, (bottom left): Shutterstock.com/Irina Bort,
(bottom middle): Shutterstock.com/oksana2010, (bottom right):
Shutterstock.com/spillikin; p. 17, back cover: iStock.com/sdominick; pp.
17 (right, bottom), 32 (top right, bottom): Shutterstock.com/Adventuring
Dave; pp. 17 (second from right), 32 (top left): iStock.com/sdominick; p.
18: Shutterstock.com/Monkey Business Images; p. 19 (top): Shutterstock.
com/Oleksandr Berh, (bottom): iStock.com/hsyncoban; p. 20: iStock.
com/skynesher; p. 21: iStock.com/mixetto; p. 22: iStock.com/fstop123; p.
23: iStock.com/monkeybusinessimages; p. 24: Shutterstock.com/Billion
Photos; p. 26: iStock.com/Amorn Suriyan; p. 27: iStock.com/Will Langston;
p. 28: iStock.com/mheim3011; p. 29: iStock.com/davit85; p. 30:
Shutterstock.com/Alena Ozerova.

Every effort has been made to trace and acknowledge copyright.
However, if any infringement has occurred, the publishers tender their
apologies and invite the copyright holders to contact them.

NovaStar

Text © 2024 Cengage Learning Australia Pty Limited

ISBN 978 0 17 033442 6

Cengage Learning Australia
Level 5, 80 Dorcas Street
Southbank VIC 3006 Australia
Phone: 1300 790 853
Email: aust.nelsonprimary@cengage.com

For learning solutions, visit **cengage.com.au**

Printed in China by 1010 Printing International Ltd
1 2 3 4 5 6 7 28 27 26 25 24

*Nelson acknowledges the Traditional Owners and Custodians
of the lands of all First Nations Peoples. We pay respect
to Elders past and present, and extend that respect to
all First Nations Peoples today.*

Contents

What Is Wellbeing?

Wellbeing is about keeping healthy, happy and safe. Our wellbeing depends on the choices we make in different parts of our life. There are many things we can choose to do to improve our wellbeing.

We can eat **nutritious** foods and be active to have a healthy body. We can try to understand our feelings so we can cope better when we make mistakes or have disappointments.

Being active is one way to stay healthy and improve our wellbeing.

We can share experiences with others and be kind and thoughtful. This helps us develop positive **relationships** with friends and family. These relationships help us feel like we belong, which is an important part of wellbeing.

Sharing experiences can help families develop positive relationships.

We also need to look after our minds. For times when we need to calm down and look after our wellbeing, we can practise some calming **techniques**.

Yoga is one calming technique we can try.

Wellbeing and the Body

Our bodies work better when they are fit and healthy. So trying to be as fit and healthy as possible is an important choice we can make for our wellbeing.

Eating Well

Eating nutritious foods gives our bodies the best chance to grow and be strong. Many foods, such as fresh fruits and vegetables, grains, **lean** meat, fish, and dairy foods, contain lots of **vitamins** and **minerals**. These substances provide our bodies with the building blocks needed to help us see well, have energy and develop strong bones, teeth and muscles.

Our wellbeing can depend on the food choices we make.

If we eat unhealthy foods, we are not making the best choice for our bodies. Fizzy drinks and snack foods like biscuits and hot chips usually contain large amounts of sugar, fat and salt. Although these snacks can taste good, they can be bad for our health and wellbeing.

Foods that contain lots of sugar and salt are not good for our bodies.

Wellbeing Tip

Choose healthy snacks, like fruit, cheese or carrot sticks, and drink plenty of water.

Being Active

Being active is good for our bodies. Exercise gives us more energy, makes our muscles stronger and can even make us happier.

When we exercise, the brain releases **endorphins**. These endorphins send signals around the body that make us feel happy and well.

Wellbeing ✳Tip✳

Aim to do some form of exercise for at least one hour each day.

Being active makes us feel happy and well.

Exercise can take many different forms, so we can choose activities that we enjoy doing. Taking a pet for regular walks or riding a bike to school are good forms of exercise. And there are many sports that we can try, from ball games to athletics. Dancing is also an enjoyable and creative way to move and be active.

Taking your pet for a walk is a great form of exercise.

Dancing is a fun way to stay active.

Switching Off Screens

We can spend a lot of time looking at screens on digital devices, like computers, tablets and TVs. Choosing to switch them off can improve our wellbeing.

Sitting and watching shows or playing video games for hours at a time can become a **habit** that is hard to break. Video games are often designed to give players rewards that encourage them to keep playing.

Too much screen time can be bad for our health and wellbeing.

But sitting at screens can stop us from doing other things, like being active and spending time with friends and family.

Looking at screens can make our eyes tired and sore. It can also make it harder to **concentrate** and even cause headaches. It can stop us from getting enough sleep, too.

When we're not looking at screens, we have more time for other things, like playing board games with our families.

Wellbeing *Tip*

Try to spend less than two hours each day looking at screens.

Getting Enough Sleep

Sleep is essential to our wellbeing because when we sleep, our muscles and our minds can rest and relax. If we don't get enough sleep, we are tired the next day, and it can be harder to remember things and learn new information.

When we don't get enough sleep, we find it hard to concentrate and learn.

During sleep, the body makes a substance called **human growth hormone**. This substance helps us to grow and also repairs any damage to our muscles and bones.

It's important to have a healthy night-time **routine** that calms the body down and prepares it for sleep. This includes turning off any screens an hour or two before bedtime. The light from screens can have the same effect on the brain as being in sunlight. The light sends signals to the brain telling it that it's time to be alert and awake.

Reading a book before bed can help us relax. Then we can fall asleep quickly and get enough sleep.

Reading a book before bed is better than looking at a screen.

Wellbeing
✲ Tip ✲

School children need between 9 and 11 hours of sleep each night to be healthy.

Wellbeing and Feelings

Our wellbeing is closely connected to our feelings. When we understand our feelings, it can help us cope with challenges and explore ways of fixing them. These include being kind to ourselves and grateful for the things we have.

Coping with Challenges

It would be nice if we could always feel happy, but sometimes we have to cope with challenges. For example, we might be upset about being put in a different class from our friends at school. Or we might be **frustrated** with ourselves for missing a goal in a sports game.

It's okay to feel upset or frustrated sometimes.

It's helpful to understand that everyone feels disappointed, annoyed or embarrassed at times in their lives. Being kind to ourselves is a good way of dealing with these feelings. That means practising positive **self-talk**. Instead of making **critical** comments to ourselves, like, "You really messed up that goal", it can be kinder to tell ourselves, "It's disappointing that I didn't get the goal, but I tried my best and I'll keep on practising."

Practising positive self-talk is a good way to cope with difficult feelings.

Wellbeing ✳ Tip ✳

Use positive self-talk to remind yourself that you are brave, and that you believe in your abilities!

Making kindness Rocks

You can make kindness rocks to help yourself remember some positive self-talk. Kindness rocks are also good presents to give to others.

Goal

To paint kind messages and pictures on rocks for yourself or others

Materials

You will need:

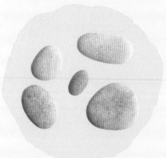

small rocks

colourful paint

thick and thin paintbrushes

Steps

1. Paint a background colour on your rock with a thick paintbrush.

2. Use a thin paintbrush to paint a picture or design on the rock.

3. Write a kind message on one or both sides of the rock.

4. Leave the rock to dry.

5. Put the rock in a room or garden, where you or someone else can read it.

6. Have fun encouraging others to be kind to themselves!

Wellbeing *Tip*

Kindness rock messages can be simple words, like "Smile" and "Happiness". Or you can think of messages to inspire, like "Rock your day" or "You've got this!"

Being Grateful

Another way to understand our feelings and improve our wellbeing is by being grateful. This means thinking about all the things we have and being thankful for them.

When we practise gratefulness, we often realise how lucky we are, even though we might feel sad or grumpy about something. We might be grateful for the family and friends who care about us. Or we might be grateful to have teachers who help us learn. We can also be grateful for simple things, like having a delicious lunch to eat.

We can be grateful for a tasty lunch or the company of a friend.

It can be helpful to create a gratefulness diary. Every day, we can write down one small thing we feel grateful for. This can also make us aware of the need to help others who are not as lucky.

All you need to practise gratefulness is a notebook and a pen.

Writing down things that we are grateful for makes us feel good.

Wellbeing and Relationships

When we have positive relationships with other people, such as family, friends and classmates, we feel like we belong. This is an important part of our wellbeing. If we understand our feelings, we can also deal with problems that sometimes happen in relationships.

Feeling Like We Belong

Having strong relationships makes our lives more fun and exciting because we get to spend time with other people and do lots of different activities. We might belong to an organised group, like a sports team, a singing group or a science club.

Being part of a group, like a singing group, can help us to feel like we belong.

Doing activities in groups can help us work together to achieve something special, such as winning a match or performing in a show. This helps us to build trusting relationships. Being part of a group also lets us see things from other people's points of view. We can learn to share our ideas, listen to others and get along with them.

Being thoughtful and kind to others can improve our relationships. Strong relationships help make us feel comfortable and safe, which adds to our wellbeing and feeling of belonging.

Wellbeing ⋆Tip⋆

Helping a parent carry some shopping or making a bracelet for a friend are some ways to be kind and thoughtful.

Handling Challenges in Relationships

Sometimes, we can have challenges in our relationships. For example, we might be angry with a friend or family member. We might say things we soon wish we hadn't. And that can upset our sense of wellbeing.

If we think about why we were angry, this can help us understand our feelings. We can then try to fix any problems in our relationships.

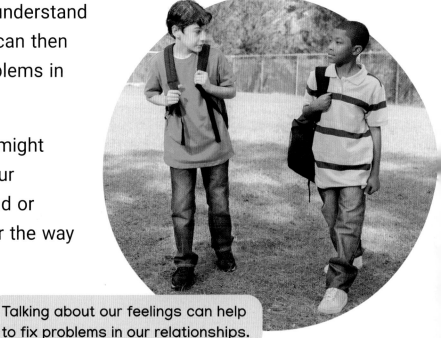

For example, we might want to explain our feelings to a friend or even say sorry for the way we behaved.

Talking about our feelings can help to fix problems in our relationships.

Wellbeing *Tip*

A simple act, like making a card, could help another person understand your feelings.

Wellbeing and the Mind

Looking after our minds is an important part of wellbeing. We can do this by learning how to calm our thoughts and **focus** on tasks.

Mindfulness and yoga are some techniques for calming the mind. They help us focus and improve our memory, as well as our health and wellbeing.

We can practise mindfulness while doing things such as taking a walk.

Mindfulness

When we practise mindfulness, we focus our mind on whatever activity we're doing at the time. This might sound simple, but sometimes we don't stop to realise that we're thinking about all sorts of different things at once. It's as if our minds are racing, and it can be hard to slow our thoughts down and concentrate on what we really need to do.

Practising mindfulness is a good way to help us slow down our thoughts.

Much of the time, we have daily habits we perform without thinking, such as eating breakfast. Or we could be trying to concentrate on reading a book. While we do these activities, we might be thinking about other things, like making sure we have packed our school bag. These thoughts can make us **anxious** and forgetful, and we can lose our concentration.

Being mindful is like exercise for the mind. It's a special way of slowing down and staying calm by cutting out all the extra thoughts. It can help us to get things done and enjoy each activity we do during our day.

Being mindful is a great way to help us stay calm.

Mindful Breathing

Breathing brings **oxygen** into our bodies. We need oxygen to stay alive. Mindful breathing calms us down by concentrating our minds on breathing deeply. This increases the flow of oxygen around the body.

Our brain reacts to the oxygen by making endorphins, which spread through the body and make us feel happy and relaxed. They can also reduce pain if we have hurt ourselves.

Sitting in a quiet place and focusing on deep breathing is good for our body and mind.

Wellbeing ★Tip★ If you feel anxious or angry during the day, just a few minutes of mindful breathing can help you feel better.

Doing Mindful Breathing

This mindful breathing exercise can calm you down if you feel anxious. It can be done sitting, lying down or even standing up. Remember to breathe in through your nose, and out through your mouth.

Goal

To calm your mind using mindful breathing

Steps

1 Relax your shoulders.

2 Breathe in deeply for 4 seconds.

3 Hold the breath for 4 seconds.

4 Slowly breathe out for 4 seconds.

5 Hold for 4 seconds.

6 Repeat two more times.

7 Notice how much calmer and more relaxed you feel, and get on with your day.

Yoga

Practising yoga is another way of moving and being mindful. Yoga involves doing different **poses** that make us more aware of the ways our body can move and stretch. The poses have names like tree, cobra, eagle and happy baby.

cobra pose

The movements in yoga are slow and steady, and are done while concentrating on the breath. Yoga is good for strengthening muscles and improving our balance, as well as calming our minds and helping us focus.

Yoga can be done inside or outside. Some schools run yoga sessions for students, and there are many places where children can learn yoga.

There are even yoga camps for children.

Wellbeing Tip

You can learn how to do some basic yoga poses from books and websites.

Wellbeing for Life

Looking after our wellbeing is not something we can do once and then forget about. It's up to us to keep on making the best choices throughout our lives to ensure our wellbeing stays in good shape.

So, we need to remember to look after our bodies and be more aware of our feelings. We can work on developing happy, positive relationships, and practise mindfulness and yoga to help us stay calm and focused. Enjoy the feeling of wellbeing!

Looking after our wellbeing makes us feel happy and connected.

Glossary

anxious (*adjective*)	nervous or worried
concentrate (*verb*)	to think about and pay attention to what you are doing
critical (*adjective*)	not approving of something or someone
endorphins (*noun*)	natural chemicals made by the body that produce happy feelings
focus (*verb*)	to pay close attention to something
frustrated (*adjective*)	tense and unhappy about something that isn't going well
habit (*noun*)	an activity that is repeated often
human growth hormone (*noun*)	a substance produced by the brain that controls bone length and muscle growth
lean (*adjective*)	containing not much fat
mindfulness (*noun*)	a practice that helps us pay attention to what is happening in the present moment
minerals (*noun*)	natural substances found in foods that are needed by the body
nutritious (*adjective*)	having lots of substances that are good for health
oxygen (*noun*)	the gas in the air that helps keep living things alive
poses (*noun*)	different ways of standing or sitting
relationships (*noun*)	connections between people such as friends or relatives
routine (*noun*)	a series of actions that are always the same
self-talk (*noun*)	talking to and about yourself in your head
techniques (*noun*)	particular ways of doing things
vitamins (*noun*)	natural substances found in foods that are important for health

Index